zendoodle coloring

Little Big Cats

Little Big Cats

Baby Wild Cats to Color and Display

illustrations by

Jeanette Wummel

CASTLE POINT BOOKS

NEW YORK

ZENDOODLE COLORING: LITTLE BIG CATS.
Copyright © 2021 by St. Martin's Press. All rights reserved.
Printed in the United States of America. For information, address
St. Martin's Publishing Group, 120 Broadway, New York, NY 10271.

www.castlepointbooks.com

The Castle Point Books trademark is owned by Castle Point Publishing, LLC.
Castle Point books are published and distributed by St. Martin's Publishing Group.

ISBN 978-1-250-27636-0 (trade paperback)

Our books may be purchased in bulk for promotional, educational, or business use.
Please contact your local bookseller or the Macmillan Corporate and Premium
Sales Department at 1-800-221-7945, extension 5442, or by email
at MacmillanSpecialMarkets@macmillan.com.

First Edition: 2021

10 9 8 7 6 5 4 3 2 1

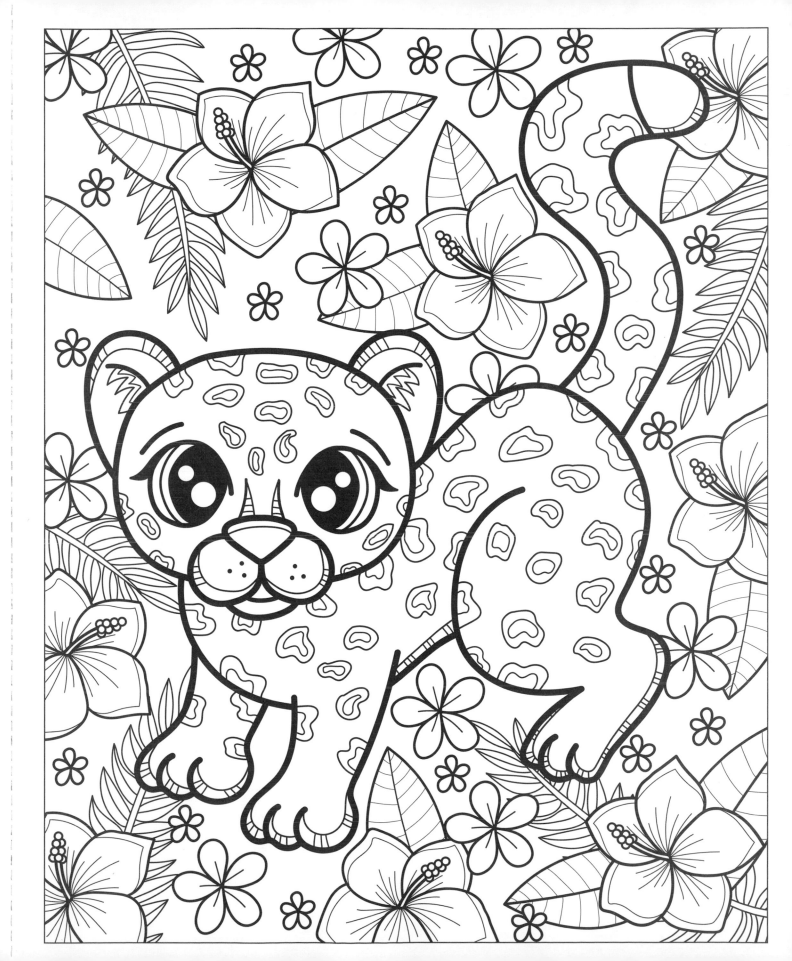